A LAKE SUPERIOR JOURNEY
by jack nordgren

I would like to dedicate this book to my spiritual
and surf mentors:

SPIRITUAL MENTORS:
George & Ethyl Nordgren
Maree Nordgren
Pastor Bob & Donna Brunko
Pastor Howard & Grace Engnell
Wally Shaw
Dr. Al Glenn
Wayne Cordero
Ralph Moore

SURF MENTORS:
Ron Harling
Monte Mansfield (Scooter)
Dennis Sallas
Virgil Sisiam

CONTACT JACK!
HCBnewsletter@aol.com
southshorefellowship.org

This book is also dedicated to my grand children:
Bethany, Savannah, Silas, & Jack....and also
to those yet to be born. May they continue this
legacy of faith to the next generations.

Book design by Salty Pineapple Design • saltypineapple.org

ACKNOWLEDGMENTS:

Writing this book was one of the hardest things I've ever done. It has taken over two years. I basically had to relive the past 30 years of my life. I literally had to go through hundreds of old pictures. I've tried to recount the events as best I could.

It was Pastor Ralph Moore who told me I should write this book. He gave me helpful tips on writing. As a Pastor, I find his counsel to be as good as you get. I had no idea what I was getting myself into.

I knew it would be a long project. I did it anyway because of something that was said to me a long time ago. Pastor Wayne Cordeiro once told me, "Don't be afraid of big projects".

My beautiful wife Maree has been by my side encouraging, helping me the whole way. She has been writing our monthly newsletters since 1978. She has become a wonderful writer and without her help this book would not have been possible.

My oldest son Jason was our editor. He did a wonderful job.

Our good friend Hans Riemenschneider at Salty Pineapple Design did the layout. His encouragement and input was invaluable.

As I sit here typing, having completed my part of this project, I have a heart filled with gratitude to my Lord and Savior Jesus Christ.

PSALM 93

[1]The Lord reigns, he is robed in majesty; the Lord is robed in majesty and is armed with strength. The world is firmly established; it cannot be moved. [2]Your throne was established long ago; you are from all eternity.

[3]The seas have lifted up, O Lord, the seas have lifted up their voice; the seas have lifted up their pounding waves. [4]Mightier than the thunder of the great waters, mightier than the breakers of the sea— the Lord on high is mighty.

[5]Your statutes stand firm; holiness adorns your house for endless days, O Lord

CONTENTS

Photo by Mike Killion

It's never too cold to surf.

A LAKE SURFER'S JOURNEY

INTRODUCTION

I T was a Saturday afternoon, late afternoon; I was cruising home on K-Highway when I noticed that the surf had just come up. There were some 15-25 knot trade winds tugging spray back, forming some perfect head high barrels. As I looked, I saw one peal off WITH NOBODY ON IT. My heart started pumping harder as I realized nothing was planned for that evening and maybe, just maybe I could surf.

As I got home, I told my wife what I had just seen and she (God, I love that woman) said, "Go for it". My son Josh was home, so as I threw my shorts on, I asked him if he'd like to join me. By the position of the sun, I figured we had a solid 45 minutes before it actually set behind the Diamond Head. After that we'd have maybe 20-30 minutes or so of twilight. "It wouldn't be the first time I would have to use the street lights to get my bearings", I thought as we paddled out.

Josh was on his boogie board and I was on my long board. I teased him about being a half surfer but inside I just felt so gosh darn proud of him. He and his best friend Aaron actually had gained a reputation at Kaiser High School as hot body boarders; 360 Jack stands and el rollos were part of their Makapu'u repertoire.

Originally being from the South Side of Chicago, I had surfed the Great Lakes. Hawaii was the last place in the world I thought I'd end up. Living seven minutes from the ocean and having consistent surf and warm water were beyond my wildest dreams. Having sons that loved the water was a blessing that was almost too much to take in.

Our stoke was halved, when we saw another surfer dropping in. We looked at each other and said, "Oh well, I guess we'll have to share". Things aren't always what they seem from the shore. This was one of those times. It was even better than we thought. The waves were overhead. There were two guys out. Imagine our disappointment when they decided to paddle in.

As the apostle Paul wrote," our joy knew no bounds". We proceeded to shred those walls of water. Hooting, laughing, sharing, surfing our brains out; we pulled out all the stops. We held nothing back. It was almost like time stood still, kinda like a magical fairy tale. We were sharing a super special place, a super special time, a super special experience. It is a treasure that we will always share.

After about 45 minutes the sun hit the mountain top. I said, "Well, we better think about going in. We don't want to paddle in, in the dark". My words met with silence. We both knew what each other were thinking, "One more wave". After another wave the same thought came in to our heads again. So we caught another wave. Each wave was better than the former. Then we caught another wave then another and another. There was only about 5 minutes of twilight left when we agreed on one more wave and really meant it.

After a few minutes of paddling in, there was no more twilight left. We now had to navigate by the lights on the shore. Hazards that were easy to spot in the daylight now posed a real threat. Razor sharp coral heads just below the surface of the water were impossible to spot. Rocks and shallows were a constant threat to our hands and boards. Most surfers would rather cut themselves than ding their precious surfboards. I was no exception; neither was Josh. He was sponging (boogie boarding) and had to be careful of his knees. It was definitely a sketchy paddle in. Our intense concentration made us put aside our glorious memories. We made it in OK with only minor cuts and abrasions and no dings. We always make it a point to pray before we paddle out. It's kinda like saying grace before a meal. Most surfers would rather surf than eat anyway so you figure it out. This was a time of being especially dependent on the Lord and prayer.

It was a few days later, I was reading my daily Psalms and Proverbs. This was a habit I picked up from my Dad and an evangelist by the name of Billy Graham. It was the 4th day of the month so I was reading Proverbs chapter 4. There are 31 chapters in the book of Proverbs. It works out to one a day, except for February and the 30 day months. On those months there is a little extra reading. Anyway, as I read Proverbs 4:18-19, a revelation exploded in my head.

Proverbs 4:18-19 "The path of the righteous is like the first gleam of dawn, shining ever brighter till the full light of day. But the way of the wicked is like deep darkness; they do not know what makes them stumble."

My life before I knew Jesus Christ as my Lord and Savior was like that evening session with Josh. My life was good but it was getting darker and darker. I couldn't see where I was going. Things weren't making sense. My life after I met Christ was like dawn patrol. My life was getting brighter and brighter. The closer I got to God the more I understood what was going on. That pretty well describes the story you are about to read, "A Lake Surfer's Journey". I hope you are blessed by reading it.

Jason Nordgren dawn patrol "Turtles" Oahu, Hawaii

CHAPTER ONE

SURF-A-HOLIC

YOU have heard of people being addicted to many different things. For instance, you have probably heard the term alcoholic, which is a person who is physically and/or psychologically dependent on the continued use of alcohol. I became an addict as well, although I was dependent on a much different type of liquid.

It all started out so innocently. I never intended to become a surf-a-holic. I just wanted to have some fun. It was the summer of my sophomore year in high school. My family was spending the summer at Bethany Beach in Sawyer, Michigan. We stayed at my grandma's house near the lake. It was like a completely different world from where we lived in Chicago.

The beach was a stone's throw from my Grandma's cottage. My summer friends and I were down there hanging out. The Harling brothers, Ron and Ted, came down to the beach. They had just gotten back from a vacation in Florida. Their parents had bought them each a surfboard. I thought they had the coolest parents in the world.

Ron Harling & Don Wichert at Ersula's St. Joe, Michigan

I had never seen surfboards up close before. They were the most beautiful things I'd ever seen. They were 9'6" with competition stripes down the middle. One was made by Hobie, the other by Miller.

We all swam out to the sandbar to watch Ron and Ted. They were actually catching waves and riding them! It was fascinating. Then came the fateful moment that changed my life forever. Ron asked me if I wanted to try. I didn't want to. I tried to swim away. They all laughed and called me chicken. I swam back. Ron pushed the surfboard towards me. I stood waiting, in waist deep water, ready to jump on the first wave. I was apprehensive. My heart was beating wildly.

As the first set came, I pushed off the sandbar, laid on the board and stroked deep into the water. I felt somewhat unstable as I stood up and went down the face of the wave...but I had caught it! What a rush! I was surfing- YEEHAA... right to the bottom. I pearled. The nose of the board shot straight down to the bottom, like a pearl diver. It was a perfect wipeout. "Good!" I thought. They won't ask me to do it again. They'll all want their turns now." It didn't work. They made me try again.

This time I wasn't so lucky. I paddled into the next wave caught it, stood up and rode it all the way to shore. The feeling was incredible. Gliding across the top of the water on a surf board is something that is hard to describe. It feels like you are defying gravity as you are flying across the surface. From that moment I was hooked. I was addicted to surfing. I lived, ate and breathed surfing. I WAS A SURF-A-HOLIC.

Some of my friends became addicted too. They had similar experiences. Some had been to the East Coast and surfed the Atlantic. Some discovered lake surfing. But all of us were hooked. We were mesmerized and in love...not with a hot girl, but with surfing. We all felt surfing was the coolest sport in the world. In fact to us it was more than a sport. It was a way of life. We started dressing differently. We started talking differently. We even thought differently. Our conversations were constantly about surfing.

I continued surfing with the Harling brothers and using their boards. But after a while, I wasn't satisfied anymore. I had to have my own board. At that time there were no surf shops on Lake Michigan (or so I thought). While browsing through a Montgomery Ward catalog I made a discovery. They had a wake board for sale.

Wake boards were designed to ride the wake behind a boat. It wasn't a surfboard, but it was close. It looked like a surfboard, except that the skeg (fin) was located farther forward and was attached with 6 wood screws.

My first board from Montgomery Ward

For those of you, who have never surfed, let me explain something. Wood screws on a surfboard, wake board or any other kind of water board are an accident waiting to happen. Lake water soaked the wood, weakened it, and caused the screws holding the skeg to start to come out.

So, within a month while Timmy Norville was borrowing my board, my skeg came off in Lake Michigan. It was never seen or heard from again. I only had just bought the board, and now it was as useless as a full wet suit in Hawaii. To say I was totally bummed would be a complete understatement.

It is almost impossible to turn a surfboard without a skeg. Actually, the ancient Hawaiian surfers could do it. They would drag their foot or hand in the water to turn their board. Once they turned though, there was no changing direction. They use to say," Set it and forget it". It takes a considerable amount of practice and skill to be able to do this. I had neither.

I tried to surf without the skeg but it was impossible for me. I was crushed. It felt like my best friend had just died. Several days later, I told Ron Harling. He just smiled and said,

"Don't worry. We'll just have to drive to Grand Haven."

"Grand Haven? Why?" I asked. Grand Haven was two hours away.

"There is a surf shop in Grand Haven," he answered.

He had seen their advertisement in Surfer Magazine. I was stoked! I could get a new skeg. I figured Grand Haven must be Grand Heaven. That two hour drive to the shop seemed like only two minutes. I would be able to surf again.

The size of the waves is determined by the velocity, direction and duration of the wind. The stronger the wind, the longer it lasts and the greater distance it blows over the lake the bigger the waves. Grand Haven is a great place to surf because of its location. Most Lake Michigan beaches can only get waves if the wind blows in one certain direction. Grand Haven can get waves on north, south or west winds, or various combinations of the three. It also has a long pier. Piers are a great advantage for lake surfers. Lake waves tend to be choppy because of the wind making the water less smooth and harder to surf. Usually one side of the pier will be choppier than the other. The other side will be cleaner, which makes it easier to surf.

Needless to say, Grand Haven was to lake surfers as Jerusalem is to the Jews. Ron and I felt like we were in a beach town on the coast, and not in the Midwest United States. There was indeed a surf shop and there were a ton of surfers. After we bought the skeg, we cruised around. We counted about 20 guys surfing at the local break. That night they had a street dance. There was a surf band with over 100 surf guys and gals hanging out. We had a blast!

We spent the night at an old hotel overlooking the lake. The next day we were awakened by a very loud fog horn. We had to remind ourselves that we were still in the Midwest.

We headed home totally stoked. I don't know if there is a surf shop there anymore, but I do know there is a great surf shop in New Buffalo, Michigan. It's called Third Coast Surf Shop. I know because I work there!

Bob Beaton - Grand Haven Michigan 1967

When I got back to Chicago I needed help to fix my board. My Dad asked his friend Ray to help me. He was a handyman so he knew a lot about everything. To be fixed properly, the skeg needed to be glassed in and reinforced with fiberglass cloth and resin. We didn't do it that way because we didn't know any better, so we improvised.

Ray used a screw again, but this time we screwed it in through the board from the top. It was not the best way to mount a skeg, but the main thing was it worked! That skeg never came out again.

I was so happy! My board was fixed. It had a brand new speed skeg which made my board even more stable at faster speeds than it was before.

I now had a surfboard, but I still dressed like a greaser. Greasers wore black pants, black shoes and black socks with white tee shirts and black leather jackets. The name greaser comes from the fact that we used to put stuff in our hair which looked like grease. It was much different from the wax and gels kids use today. We were a lot like "the Fonz" from Happy Days. Our hair was greased back and if you were really cool, you had a ducktail in the front. A ducktail looks like the tail of a duck lying down on your forehead. It was very cool for greasers, but not for surfers.

The next summer found me at Camp Hickory in Round Lake, Illinois. I was working as a dishwasher. It was there that I was confronted with my hypocrisy. The two camp lifeguards dressed like surfers. They introduced me to white Levis, madras shirts, and penny loafers with no socks. I was told this was the appropriate surfer attire. As soon as I could, I purchased a new wardrobe and washed the grease out of my hair. I was now officially a surfer!

In 1966, I was the only surfer in my high school. Most of the guys in my school were greasers. This one guy used to ask me if they could take up a collection for me...you know, to buy me some socks. I was teased all the time. I didn't care because I was a surfer. I was cool. I had the board, I had the new skeg, and now I had the clothes.

I not only surfed but I was into anything that even resembled surfing. I had a wooden skate board with clay wheels. Downhill roads, wet grassy hills, snowy slopes...I rode them all. At a winter Y.M.C.A. camp I was the first one to ride a snurf board (the forerunner of snowboards) without holding on to the rope. It was like surfing except on snow. I wonder if that makes me the father of snowboarding? Maybe it qualifies me for some royalties. That would be totally gnarly (very extreme)!

In the summer of 1967, after graduating from Fenger High School in Chicago, I rented a room in a beach house in St. Joe Michigan. The rent was $20 a week. There wasn't a lot of surf at St. Joe, but it was on the beach.

My friends and I surfed whenever we could. When there were waves, all other plans and activities went on hold. It was there I had the most incredible surf experience of my life thus far.

Jack Nordgren - Ersula's – St. Joe, Michigan 1967

It was a Friday night. As was our custom, my friends and I were having a party on the beach. The wind was blowing out of the west. It was straight on shore and huge waves were rolling in.

Although the waves were big, they would be difficult to ride. The wind was blowing behind them and making them messy. The best waves are like long lines. These waves were the opposite. They were disorganized short peaks, totally gnarly and unrideable. Just about the time the party broke up we took one last look at the surf. We noticed that the wind had shifted. It was now blowing off shore.

Instead of making the waves choppy, the wind was blowing onto the front of the waves. It was giving them better shape and making them smoother. It was going to make for some of the best lake surf possible. None of us had ever seen conditions as good as this before.

We stayed on the beach to watch. At 4 a.m. we could just barely make out A-frame waves. Usually waves break best either right or left but not both ways. A-frames break good either way, which means you can ride which ever way you want. My friend Clay Carlson and I got our boards. We sat on the beach and waited for the sun.

At the first glimmer of daylight, we paddled out. The waves were peeling off and breaking in both directions. They were perfection. We caught a few. This was the best surf I had ever experienced so far! I was stoked! I was ready to burst... and then it got even better!

I paddled for another wave and dropped in. As I stood up and turned right I noticed this wave was different from the others. It started to bowl up in front of me. It felt like a circle of water was surrounding me without touching me. I crouched down so the lip of the wave wouldn't hit me in the head. All of a sudden, everything around me was white. It was like I was in a white room. The wave had totally covered me without knocking me off my board. Suddenly, I was out and there was sky. I paddled back out to the line-up. We sat in silence for a few minutes.

Clay broke the spell. "Did you just get tubed?" he asked.

"Yeah, I think I did." Then the reality of what happened set in. "Wait, I know I did!" We both yelled and hooted. We celebrated like we had both been in that barrel together.

Getting barreled (tubed) is the ultimate experience in surfing. Surfers always try to stay as close to the curl (white water) as possible. That's where the wave is the most powerful. When you get barreled, you are as close to the power as you can get. The wave breaks in a circle over you and it pushes you forward while it is breaking. There is a wall of water on every side of you, but you are not getting wet! Some surfers call it "being in the green room" or "the blue room" as the blue-green water envelops you without touching your body. It is a total rush! It's a natural high!

Ron Harling, Duane & Chuck Perkins

My first surfari (major surf trip) to the East Coast also happened that summer. Ron Harling's 1964 Volkswagen van went to the Jersey shore. It was loaded with me, Ron, Vince, Chuck and Dwayne. We only had three 8 track tapes to listen to. I could handle Canned Heat and Simon & Garfunkel, but I hated Cream. We listened to those tapes over and over and over. By the end of the trip, Cream had become one of my favorite bands.

This was to be the first of many surfaris. We surfed different spots from Long Island, New York all the way down to Cocoa Beach, Florida. We had many great adventures and forged friendships that have lasted a lifetime. Some of the guys were totally addicted like me. There was Clay Carlson (Ace King Goum) and his brother Kenny (the King). Clay worked with some guys who like to use the nick-name Ace King Goum. We liked the name so much we gave it to him. Kenny got his nickname on a surfari with my wife and me. My wife said," All Kenny does is sleep, surf and eat. He acts like he's a king". The name stuck.

Other friends of mine were able to function normally in society like John, Dwight, Erik and Peter. They had been exposed to surfing but somehow were able to resist the pull of the waves. They had the strength and inner fortitude to press on and lead normal lives. The rest of us had lives that revolved around surfing. Normal activities, like going to work, dates with girlfriends or family gatherings were always in danger of getting canceled or postponed by the surf coming up.

My first surfari was also my first taste of the ocean, literally. In Lake Michigan we surfed in fresh water. You can drink lake water, but it's not recommended.

The ocean is a different story. Basically, salt water is 2 1/2% more dense than fresh water. Although the water is too salty to be drinkable, it's more buoyant than fresh water. It's kinda like you lost a few pounds. You just float better.

Ocean waves are also more powerful, faster and spaced further apart than lake waves. This makes for a quicker, more intense experience while surfing. For a lake surfer to surf in the ocean for the first time is a really big deal. It's like a minor league baseball athlete playing in the World Series.

Everything about the ocean is magnified. The power of the waves and the way they break is more intense than lake waves. The Atlantic Ocean took some getting used to for this lake surfer. But after a few sessions I was in the zone and surfing like a natural.

Surfers tell each other all the time how the waves were. "It was so much bigger...you should have been here an hour ago," is a typical greeting to a surfer just paddling out into the lineup. I was always in search of the perfect wave, but I could never seem to find it. The perfect wave was always elusive. It seemed just beyond my reach.

Chuck Perkins at Clark Street Beach – Evanston, Illinois 1967

I had become a surf-a-holic. Surfing had become my religion. I had been raised a Christian. I believed in God. But now I was worshipping the creation rather than the Creator.

During this time I was far from my Creator, but He wasn't far from me. My Aunt Ruth and my folks were praying for me. I was oblivious to it. As far as I was concerned, life was good. I was a surfer and I didn't have a care in the world.

But two things were about to change that. The first was the war in Vietnam (1968), and the other was the military draft.

CHAPTER TWO

THE GNARLY YEARS

Gnarly (surfer's definition) – extremely dangerous, huge, unreliable to ride, taking your life into your own hands.

During high school, I was never sure about what to do with my life. After graduation, I really wasn't interested in going to college. Now I had some serious motivation. The motivation came from the military draft. I knew that there was a good chance I'd be drafted. The government prevented college students from being drafted. So, I enrolled in Loop Jr. College in downtown Chicago. I knew that it only took 12 credit hours a semester to get a deferment. What I didn't know was that I needed 30 credit hours for the year. So, at the end of my first year, I was 6 hours short. This meant I was now eligible in Uncle Sam's eyes to be drafted into the military. There was now a good chance I would be sent to Vietnam.

I got my draft notice. My number was low....52. This meant that I would be drafted within a few months by the Army, and would probably be headed for Viet Nam. Not wanting to go there, I enlisted in the Navy. Vietnam was a war being fought on the ground and in the jungle, swamps, and rivers.

Actually, I had always wanted to join the Navy. My Dad was on a LCI landing craft in WWII. I had grown up listening to his Navy stories. Some were tall tales he told to me as bed-time stories (like the one about stopping the Japanese torpedo with his right leg), but some were actually true. Whenever a navy movie came on the T.V. Dad would let me stay up late and watch it with him. I loved watching those movies with my dad.

It was 1969. The country was in upheaval. I volunteered for submarines and was assigned to the U.S.S. George C. Marshall. It was a Polaris submarine carrying 16 nuclear missiles. I, along with most of the military personnel, was blamed for the war. Many Americans did not want the US to be there. All over the country there were anti-war demonstrations and riots.

SSBN George C Marshall – somewhere in the Atlantic Ocean

Everyone knew we were in the military. Our haircuts gave us away. People taunted us and blamed us. I was never ashamed of serving my country. I was on active duty for almost two years and spent over 5 months submerged. None of us on that sub had any say about the war in Vietnam. We just felt like we took the blame for the politicians. They had put us there.

Drugs, sex, and rock and roll, accompanied those gnarly years. Some of my friends and I had begun experimenting with marijuana and other illegal substances. Drug use in the Navy was rampant. I remember watching some of the guys from California wandering around the barracks at 3 a.m...They were tripping out on acid, waking every body up. They had a two word vocabulary: "wow" and "dude".

Some of the crew on my sub were using drugs. I was one of them. We tried not to think about all of the fire power on our sub. One Polaris submarine had all the fire power of every bullet and every bomb from WWII, including Hiroshima and Nagasaki, and was powerful enough to destroy 16 cities of 50,000 people.

We got high to forget. Some of my friends even smoked joints right next to the charcoal air filters on board the sub. They worked pretty well in hiding their illicit activities!

There were 4 events that took place in those two years that had a huge impact on my life.

The first was that I married my childhood sweetheart. Her name was Maree McKinnis. We met at a church roller skating event when we were only twelve. We quickly became boyfriend and girlfriend. Much to my chagrin, her initial infatuation with me lasted only a month. We remained friends all through high school and found ourselves falling in love in our early twenties.

We married right before I went out on my first submarine patrol. We moved to Connecticut where I was stationed and soon afterwards, I went out to sea.

Photo by Bob Hamlett

Jack & Maree Nordgren November 14, 1970

The second event happened while I was on my first patrol, Janis Joplin died of a drug overdose. She was one of my heroes. I looked up to her for her amazing musical talent.

The third and fourth events happened while I was out at sea as well. Jimi Hendrix, another one of my heroes, died while I was making my 2nd patrol. It was reported that he, too, died of a drug overdose.

During my 3rd patrol, Jim Morrison of the 'Doors' over-dosed and died. I was stunned. I couldn't help but think that "Someone" was trying to get my attention. I began to look at the way I was living. Drugs and alcohol were a way of life, but they had taken the lives of three of my heroes in the space of a year and a half. I remember feeling the conviction of the Holy Spirit even though I was hundreds of feet below the ocean's surface.

Psalm 139:7-9 "Where can I go from your presence? Where can I flee from your Spirit? If I go up to the heavens you are there. If I make my bed in the depths you are there. If I rise on the wings of the dawn and settle on the far side of the sea you are there."

Many of my friends got to the place where they couldn't handle being in the Navy any more. They collaborated and started turning each other in, ratting each other out about their drug use. This made my life very precarious. I was being watched. I didn't want to get busted.

It turns out that I was discharged early due to health prob-lems. My asthma began acting up while we were out at sea. I was so thankful to finally get my separation papers. I didn't even care that I was leaving the coast and heading back to Chicago.

I had wanted to stay on the East Coast to surf. I had found a great surf spot in Matunik, Rhode Island. It was only 55 minutes from where we lived in Connecticut. When Maree and I were there, I was on patrol 6 months out of the year. So I had 6 months to surf. The spring and fall brought the best surf. As luck would have it, that's when I was in port.

Matunik, Rhode Island 1972

I hated giving up those long, long lefts. Being a goofy footer (a surfer who stands with their right foot forward), it was like heaven. Goofy footers like left-breaking waves because they end up facing the wave as they ride it. Maree could be very persuasive and she was not going to stay on the East Coast where we had no relatives. Our families were in Chicago and that is where she wanted to go. We moved.

Clay Carlson at Sea Isle City, New Jersey 1972

I actually found some decent surf nearby in Whiting, Indiana. It worked well on N/NE winds. I surfed there from 1973-1978. Of course, my friends and I made road trips to surf whenever we could. We went on surfaris to Rhode Island, Long Island, Cape Hatteras, and New Jersey. One time, we even drove 21 hours straight through to Florida. We had only 3 days to surf. I didn't mind. I was still a surf-a-holic.

Photo by Clay Carlson

Jack Nordgren at Cape May, New Jersey 1972

Another time my wife wanted me to stay home from going on another surfari. She was saying something about being 8 1/2 months pregnant. I thought it was only 7 1/2 months. I went anyway. Luckily she did not give birth before I got home.

Jack, Dwight, Kenny, Paul & John camping while on surfari

Not being around my Navy buddies, and being married; my drug use tapered off. I was still drinking pretty heavy, and my wife and I loved to go out drinking and dancing. We liked to party...that is, until I woke up to that gnarliest of mornings ever.

One early Sunday morning, she opened the blinds of our bedroom apartment. The sunlight hit my head like a ton of bricks. "Get up! We're going to church," she said.

"Go to hell", I answered. I put the pillow over my head.

"Get up! We're going to church or I'm getting a lawyer!"

"Whoa! Something is really, really wrong. I must have messed up," I thought. Then through tears my wife showed me her bruises...bruises that I had inflicted upon her legs. Slowly but surely she recounted the events that had led up to this. We had been out partying with friends the night before. We thought there would be dinner and drinks but there weren't.

They had only served pretzels and Seagram's 7 and 7-UP. I had gotten so blitzed that I got lost in my own neighborhood. After stumbling to our apartment I fell into bed. The room began spinning faster and faster.

I got up to go into the bathroom...or so I thought. It turns out I was on my hands and knees with my arms stretched out around the toilet bowl. Only, I was in the bedroom and my hands were gripping thin air. I began to hurl on the bedroom carpeting.

My wife grabbed the back of my shirt and tried to pull me into the bathroom. In my mind I was already there. Swearing at her I began to hit her across her legs, over and over again.

It wasn't easy for me to find out what had happened. I was so ashamed. I was so sorry. How could I have done this? My father had drilled it into me to never, ever, under any circumstances hit a woman.

So, I got up and went to church with her. It was the only time in my life that I wore sunglasses in church. My eyes were swollen. They had those red lines running through them like you see on road maps.

I thought marrying my childhood sweet heart would bring happiness. I thought surfing would always be the greatest joy of my life. Neither of them was working. I was at the lowest point of my life.

Time went on. I couldn't sleep at night. One desperate night, not knowing what else to do I opened my Bible. Like many things I've done in my life, I started backwards. I couldn't sleep. I needed God's peace. I turned to the book of Revelation, the last book in the Bible. I read all 22 chapters. Let me just say right here that if you're running from God, looking for His peace, and you want a good night's sleep, DO NOT READ Revelation! Reading about world-wide cataclysmic disaster, a 7-headed dragon, and over half the earth's population wiped out, does not bring peaceful sleep.

A few nights later, I decided to try again. This time I read the book of Matthew. I was fascinated by the life of Jesus. His life was sinless, perfect, powerful, and loving. There was no hypocrisy in Him.

Hypocrites in the church had always been my excuse for not following God. As a young teen I saw many examples in my church. They said one thing but did another. Now, I came face to face with the Son of God. Knowing about the Bible and Jesus was one thing. Knowing Jesus was something totally different.

I was reading along, starting to feel a whole lot better when I read a verse that stopped me cold. I couldn't read any further. I read Matthew 10:32, 33. Jesus said, "If you confess me before men, I will confess you before my Father in heaven. But if you deny me before men, I will deny you before my Father in heaven."

I tried to read the next verse. I couldn't. I tried a second and a third time. No matter how hard I tried, I couldn't get to the next verse. Thinking back, I remembered all the times I had tried to make a commitment to the Lord, but didn't. Then I heard the Lord. He said, "I am going to give you one more chance."

Kneeling, my prayer went something like this: "Lord, I tried this before and it didn't work but I'll give it one more try. I don't know if being a Christian will work for me but I'm willing to take a chance. If you take me, I will give my life to You."

I waited for the lightning to strike. Nothing happened. But, I slept great. It was the best night's sleep I ever had. The book of Matthew sure makes a better sleep aid than the book of Revelation.

❧

CHAPTER THREE

THE ULTIMATE SACRIFICE – MY SURFBOARD

A SURFER and his board are like God and Jesus. They are one. The surfer gets to a point where he doesn't think about how to surf. He operates on autopilot. He knows his board and how it responds. He shifts into automatic as soon as he hits the water. So, what would lead a surf-a-holic to give God his surf board? Read on. Here's how it happened.

It was Labor Day weekend. It was 1974 and it was a Saturday. This was our busiest day at True Value Hardware. My dad owned the store and I was the junior partner. Saturday's business was our bread and butter. We weren't opened on Sundays. We went to church.

Photo by Charlie Ammeson

Jack Nordgren - St. Joe, Michigan

By now, I had become a Christian, but more changes were on the way. This particular day I was asking, requesting, pleading, and begging my dad to be let off early. I had been keeping my eye on the flag at the bank, across the parking lot from the store. The winds had been 15-25 mph out of the northwest all day. I knew there were going to be waves just an hour or so away in Michigan. Dad got so frustrated with me that he finally gave in. I headed out the door at 3 p.m.

By the time I got there my friends were all surfed out. I paddled out alone. It was a near perfect day. Shoulder high sets were breaking on the second sandbar. I should have been happy but I wasn't. I felt empty and very alone. Sitting out in the line-up all by myself, I realized two things: I was sketched (feeling scared and unsure) and I was lonely.

The waves were bigger than I was used to. I had asked Jesus into my life, but He wasn't my Lord. My surf board was my god. I was still a surf-a-holic.

I didn't stay out long.

Jack Nordgren at Ersula's 1967

The next day was Sunday. I was in charge of teaching the college age class at our church. That particular Sunday, I had asked Mrs. Elkins to teach. This little old lady was anointed and powerful. She had a ministry at Cook County jail. She would go in that place and preach. If the prisoners started to act up she would tell them to "be quiet", and they would!

I'm sure she taught a good lesson that day to my class. However, I didn't hear one word. I was under deep, deep conviction. The Holy Spirit was trying to get me to do something. I knew what it was, and I didn't want to do it.

When the class ended I asked 'Mrs. E' and my wife to stay behind. We sat down in some old stuffed chairs. To this day, I still remember the musty smell.

"I want you to pray with me."

"About what?" they asked.

I struggled to speak. "I want to give Jesus my surf board."

My wife knew exactly what was going on. Mrs. E. knew, too. She sensed in her spirit that God was doing something big. "Jesus," I said through tears, "I want to give you my surf board." The tears came and I was sobbing uncontrollably. My body was convulsing with emotion. I felt like 1,000 pounds was being lifted off of me. I went home and put my surf board up in the rafters of the garage.

I truly thought that I would never surf again. Over the next few weeks I got closer and closer to God. It was great. I missed surfing but my new found peace and joy were better than anything I'd ever felt while surfing.

JESUS GIVES MY SURF BOARD BACK

I'll never forget catching the weather report one night. It was north/northeast winds 15-25 mph. "Lord, its perfect conditions for Whiting, but, I'm not going. You're first, Lord."

I couldn't help but shake this feeling that God wanted me to go. I struggled with it. The feeling persisted. "O.K. Lord", I prayed, "if you want me to go surfing then wake me up at exactly 6 a.m. I didn't set the alarm. I went to sleep.

My eyes flew open that morning. I looked at the clock. It was exactly six in the morning....not a second before and not a second after. "O.K. Lord! Let's go!" I got my board and headed out. It was about a 30 minute drive.

The waves were perfection. As I paddled out I had such a strong sense of God's peace. I could feel His presence. I was surfing alone but I wasn't lonely. The surf was almost identical to what I had experienced on Labor Day but everything else about it was so different. Jesus, the Creator of the universe wasn't far away. He was right there with me. I sensed His pleasure and delight as we surfed together.

I learned a lot that day. God wants me to do what He created me to do...surf....as long as I keep it in proper perspective. It is not to come before Him, my wife or family, my work, or my ministry responsibilities.

Here's the kicker: I actually enjoy surfing more now than ever before. I have a relationship with the Creator of the waves. I don't know if my surfing has actually improved, but it sure feels like it has.

Chuck Perkins Ocean City, New Jersey

THE BAPTISM IN THE HOLY SPIRIT

Things between me and God were good but they were about to get better. I was now reading my Bible every day. I couldn't get enough. I would spend time reading and praying every day before work. I loved God. I loved my family. I loved God's people. I loved surfing, but something was still missing from my life.

It was the mid-1970's and the Jesus Movement was happening all over the U.S. There was a revival spreading throughout the nation, but we didn't know it at the time. We just knew that God was moving big time in the south suburbs of Chicago.

My wife and I ran into a guy we knew from high school days. His name was Larry Guttman. He had been a big time drug dealer and greaser and I wanted absolutely nothing to do with him. Imagine my surprise when I bumped into him at a Christian concert. He was smiling and hugging me and asking, "Have you spoken in tongues, yet?"

"No, the Bible says, 'not all speak in tongues" I replied.

"Yes they do! You'll see", he said over his shoulder as he ran off.

"What a fruit cake!" I thought. "He's in with some real weirdoes."

We had a Christian book rack in the gift section at the hardware store. I started meeting some interesting people that were coming in to purchase the Bibles and Christian books. I was intrigued by their love for Jesus. Each time they came into the store we would have great fellowship. I found out they were "charismatic Catholics". I didn't think Catholics could even get saved! They, too, talked about tongues and something called the "baptism in the Holy Spirit."

Jack Nordgren at Ersula's St. Joe, Michigan 1967

I began seeking God. Was there more? As I read through the book of Acts I realized something. The Christians in the book of Acts had the power of the Holy Spirit. This allowed them to speak in tongues, heal people, and cast out demons. These new friends of mine were living in the book of Acts! I wasn't. They had something I didn't and I wanted it.

One morning, on my way to work, I pulled into an empty church parking lot. I turned off my van's engine and crawled into the back to kneel down. I began to pray, "Lord, I don't care what you call it... the filling of the Holy Spirit or the baptism of the Spirit, I just want all that you have for me; in Jesus name, amen."

I waited for something to happen. It didn't. I got back into the front seat and drove. As I came up to a stoplight, the Holy Spirit fell on me. I began weeping and praying. I prayed for everyone I could think of who didn't know Jesus personally.

Jesus put so much love in me, I was overflowing. I truly experienced John 7:38-39. "If you believe in me, (Jesus) come and drink! For the Scriptures declare that rivers of living water will flow out from within. When he said 'living water', he was speaking of the Spirit, who would be given to everyone believing in him. But the Spirit had not yet been given, because Jesus had not yet entered into his glory." (New Living Translation)

Joshua, Jason and Jack Nordgren in Hawaii 1980

I began witnessing to people at the hardware store. That day, I even went out and bought gospel tracts. I used my last $5.00 which was my lunch money. That same day I found $20 at work! I had never found that much money on the floor of the store and I never did again.

During my lunch hours I would drive to a nearby shopping mall to hand out the tracts and witness for Jesus. I wasn't the same person. I was experiencing the power explained in Acts 1:8 "But you shall receive power after you receive the Holy Spirit and you shall be my witnesses both in Jerusalem, Judea, and Samaria, and to the uttermost parts of the earth."

One time, I was on my way to hand out tracts and I heard that the temperature with the wind chill was -25 degrees. "I can't go. It's too cold." I thought. Then the Lord reminded me about the time I had surfed in a snow storm.

Joshua Nordgren Huntington Beach, California 2005

The weather report had been for northwest winds, 15-25 mph. I got up at 3:30 a.m. and drove to New Buffalo Michigan. I met King Kenny there. I think we only had one wet suit between us, so I went first. The waves were choppy. I was on the north side of the break water. I did manage to catch a few waves but it was pretty nuts. I only lasted about an hour. Right in the middle of the session it started to snow!

So, if I could surf in a snow storm, I could hand out tracts in -25 degrees. I put on thermal underwear and extra clothing. I was amazed at how many people came up to me to get those tracts. They must have figured I had something important to give away in that frigid weather. I did.

I hadn't spoken in tongues but I knew I had been baptized in the Holy Spirit. It would be several months later before I would begin to pray in tongues. But first, I needed to understand two important things.

Joshua Nordgren Huntington Pier, 2005

The first thing I needed to know was that there are two kinds of tongues written about in the New Testament. There is a prophetic gift of tongues that needs interpretation. "...Still another person is given the ability to speak in unknown languages, and another is given the ability to interpret what is being said." I Corinthians 12:10. Then, there is also a gift of praying in tongues or singing in tongues. "For if I pray in tongues..." I Corinthians 14:14a.

Secondly, I needed to understand that praying in tongues was actually my spirit praying and not my mind. "For if I pray in tongues, my spirit is praying, but I don't understand what I am saying. Well then, what shall I do? I will do both. I will pray in the spirit, and I will pray in words I understand. I will sing in the spirit, and I will sing in words I understand." I Corinthians 14:14, 15.

I was also dealing with fear. I feared that what I was experiencing might be coming from the devil and not from God. There was a story circulating about a foreign missionary. He was in a church where someone stood up and spoke in tongues. He recognized the dialect and realized that the person was actually blaspheming God. The enemy really used this story to bring a stronghold of fear into my life.

One night, as I was seeking God, I prayed, "Lord, I want ALL you have for me; even praying in tongues." As I drifted off to sleep, still in prayer, words started spewing out of my mouth. They were words I had never heard before.

I had been told by some Christians not to seek the gift of tongues because it was the least of all the gifts of the Spirit. That's a bit like not opening up one of your Christmas presents because it comes in a small box!

Giving my surfboard to Jesus really wasn't the ultimate sacrifice. He gave me way more than I gave Him. So many things had now been set into motion. Things that were beyond my wildest dreams were yet to come.

CHAPTER FOUR

THE CALL TO HAWAII

I T was 10:30 p.m. My wife was sleeping. I was alone watching the 700 Club. Pat Robertson was interviewing a guy from Hawaii. His name was Bob Turnbull. He talked about the beach and street ministry he had started in Waikiki.

Waikiki

"Yeah, right," I thought. "Everyone wants to go to Hawaii." He went on to explain how they had church on the beach each Sunday. He had been a youth pastor in Waikiki in a church that towered above the city. Every Sunday morning as he looked out his church's windows he saw hundreds of people on the beach; people who were not in church. He felt God was leading him to bring the church to the people and the Waikiki Beach Chaplaincy was born

He started a Sunday morning service on the beach right in front of the Hilton Hawaiian Village Hotel. The service is still going on there every Sunday! He also began a street ministry; reaching out to the visitors and locals who jammed the busy streets of Waikiki.

Photo by Bud Hamlin

Nordgren Family 1978 Chicago

"Wow! The beach and street ministry are my two favorite things. I'm already surfing on the lake and handing out tracts at the mall!" At that moment I heard the voice of the Holy Spirit speak to me that I was going. "No way," I thought.

Now, I didn't have a lot of experience with hearing God's voice. I wasn't sure if it was God or just me. Then I had this thought, "Wait, what if this really is God? O.K. Lord, if you want me to go to Hawaii, I will. However, there is one small problem. Maree isn't a Christian, yet. If you want me to go, You'll need to change her."

I didn't tell anyone about this. Several months later my Dad asked me if Maree and I would like to go to Bill Gothard's "Basic Youth Conflicts" Seminar. I told him we couldn't afford it. He told me he'd pay for it and give me the time off of work with pay.

The seminar ran from Monday through Thursday evenings with all day Friday and Saturday sessions. It was an awesome experience. We received basic, simple Bible teachings on how to live. God began growing me and healing Maree.

My wife needed healing before she could give her life to God. Her father died when she was pregnant with our first son, Jason. She was angry at God for taking her Dad so early and cheating our sons out of a grandfather. One of the things she learned at this seminar was to be thankful for the years she'd had with her dad. She needed to focus on those good memories. Focusing on what she didn't have only made her bitter.

I'll never forget the illustration Bill Gothard used. Suppose a man came down your street everyday. He would stop at each house and hand out a $100 bill. Then, one day, he passed your house. He had given everyone else the money but he passed you by.

So, you come out of your house screaming, "Hey! Where is my $100?" The point was that the money was a gift. The man didn't have to give it to you. It was not something you were entitled to. It was his to give or not to give.

As the illustration sunk in, Maree realized that the time she had been given with her Dad was a gift from God. She prayed a prayer with Bill Gothard. God touched her right then and she was healed of the resentment that she had been holding on to.

On Thursday night the talk was about demons. It was scary stuff. I felt like my wife might need some deliverance. I was scared. I didn't even want to think about it. But we were being taught that as Christians we had authority, in Jesus name, over demons.

We pulled up to the house and sat in the van, talking about what we had just learned. Maree admitted that she might need some deliverance. She had a terrible temper and struggled with uncontrollable fits of rage. We were both afraid she might actually cause harm to our little boys.

I was scared but I applied what I learned. "In the name of Jesus, I command you, satan, to come out of her." I prayed. All of a sudden my body began to tingle. I could feel the evil spirit come out of her and pass right through me. It was weird.

The next night the teaching was all about having the assurance of salvation. Mr. Gothard asked everyone to close their eyes in prayer. Then, he asked those people to raise their hands if they wanted to pray and ask Jesus into their lives. Maree raised her hand. I know because I peeked.

We were holding hands as she prayed. I was totally stoked to know that we'd be together forever in heaven. Our tears flowed. At the end of the prayer, both our arms were totally soaked in our tears.

I remembered my prayer for God to change her if he wanted me to go to Hawaii. I figured this would be as good a time as any to tell her all about it. "Honey, God has called us to Hawaii," I said, excitedly.

Jason & Joshua learning to boogie board at Waikiki Beach - 1982

That great woman of faith looked at me for a long moment and replied, "Have a good time." She had no intention of going to Hawaii or anywhere for that matter. For years she had struggled with giving her life to Christ because she was afraid that He might call her to be a pastor's wife or a missionary. She had no desire to be either. It was her worst fear. Now, it seemed it might be coming true.

While she didn't embrace our call to Hawaii right then, she did begin to grow spiritually. She started to devour her Bible. She wanted to read it and she read it often. She had a lot of questions.

One day, she came into our bedroom with her Bible opened to Acts 8:17. She read it aloud to me. "Then Peter and John placed their hands on them, and they received the Holy Spirit."

A Lake Surfer's Journey

"Would you lay hands on me? I want you to pray for me to be baptized in the Holy Spirit." she said. I prayed for her and headed to the bathroom. I really didn't expect anything to happen.

We lived in an old house. The bathroom was poorly designed. Anyone 'sitting on the throne' ran the risk of getting hit in the leg, when someone opened the door. Well, all of a sudden, I got hit in the leg.

Jason's daughter Bethany on boogie board Waikiki - 1997

I looked up into the face of my wife. Her face was radiant. Tears were flowing from her eyes. She was smiling from ear to ear. She had just been baptized in the Holy Spirit.

She was on fire for God but she still didn't want to go to Hawaii. However, she did get to the point where she said if God wanted us to go, He would have to change her heart.

That is exactly what happened. It took a year and it happened gradually. Eventually, both of us were excited about the call to Hawaii. One of the Scriptures God gave us during this time was Genesis 12:8, "By faith Abraham, when God called him to go to a place he would later receive as his inheritance, obeyed and went, even though he did not know where he was going."

That sure described us. We were called to a place and we didn't know where we were going. Neither of us had ever been there. All that we knew about Hawaii was from watching "Hawaii 5-0" on television.

I began seeking and asking the Lord on when we should go. One morning, during my prayer time, God spoke. "You're leaving one year from today." He said. The date was August 28, 1977. As I came upstairs into the kitchen Maree noticed my countenance and asked me what had happened.

"God just spoke to me and told me we are leaving a year from today."

"Wow, are you sure?"

My Dad - George Nordgren

"Yes, but don't tell anyone. I'm waiting for a confirmation."

Later that day Maree got a phone call from her friend, Leah. "Do you know when you're leaving for Hawaii?" she asked.

"Yes," Maree replied. "But Jack said he's waiting for a confirmation."

"I know when you're going," Leah said. "You're leaving one year from today."

It's hard to put into words how we felt. We were excited, blessed, scared, and full of joy. The God of the universe had spoken to us. He even told us the day we were to leave Chicago. A lot happened between August 28, 1977 and August 28, 1978.

We contacted the Waikiki Beach Chaplaincy. We told them God was calling us to join them. They told us we needed to fill out an application. If we were accepted we would then need to raise our own support. This meant that they would not pay us, and we had to have other churches and individuals send us money to live on as we worked in the ministry. They also let us know that the cost of living was about 30% higher in Hawaii than it was in the "mainland", as Hawaii locals call the contiguous 48 states.

We went from the mountain top to the valley of the shadow. We had 2 sons by now. With Jason and Joshua we were now a family of four. How would we raise support? It seemed impossible. We were literally numb.

Just then the phone rang. It was my dad. I shared with him what we had just found out. He didn't know it at the time, but he prophesied. He said, "Yes, it's impossible, but ALL things are possible with God." Hope began to grow in our hearts again. Maree found two scriptures that would become life-lines for us that next year. Psalm 37:4-5 says, "Delight yourself in the Lord and He will give you the desires of your heart. Commit your way to the Lord trust in Him and He will do this." Proverbs 3:5, 6 reads "Trust in the Lord with all your heart and lean not on your own understanding. In all your ways acknowledge Him and He will direct your paths."

We sent out a letter to everyone we knew. We shared how the Lord was leading us to the Waikiki Beach Chaplaincy. We asked them to "prayerfully consider supporting us in this ministry."

If you live on the south side of Chicago and God calls you to Hawaii, be ready. You need to steel yourself for a variety of responses when asking people to support you. Some people thought we had lost our minds. Others encouraged us. An old friend of the family even offered us money NOT to go. He thought going half-way around the world with small children was just crazy.

One cold day in January I called the pastor of a nearby church to explain about the call on our lives and to ask for help, financially. He thought it was a joke. He had just shoveled out his driveway. He said, "Who is this, really?" He thought someone in his church was playing a practical joke on him!

One thing we learned through all of this was to expect the unexpected. We received a wonderful letter of encouragement and a $500 check from an older woman, Rosalyn DeBoer. She was a widow on a fixed income.

By July 1, 1978 we had only $4000 raised and our house hadn't sold. We had less than 2 months to go, and needed a lot more money. We kept praying. We kept trusting. Then a miracle happened. Money started coming in from all over the place. We were blown away, amazed and stunned. By the end of July over $10,000 had come in. By August 28th all of our support, moving expenses, and plane tickets were covered.

Our house sold just three weeks before we left, but we still needed to sell our camper van.

I was still working for my dad at the hardware store. Saturday was my last day at work. We were leaving for Hawaii on Monday. I had a sign in the van's window. The sign read, "For Sale. See Jack in True Value Hardware."

Dad had asked me to drive across town to another True Value store and pick up some stock. I was there for only a few minutes. A customer came into the store and asked for Jack. I didn't even look up. No one knew me in this neighborhood. He asked again, "Is there a guy named Jack in here that has a van for sale?"

"That's me!" I yelled.

"Well, I'd like to buy your van," he said. I couldn't help but remember that verse from Proverbs, "and He shall direct your paths."

Nordgren Family, 1980 Waikiki

A Lake Surfer's Journey

It was a tearful but joyful departure at O'Hare airport. There were about 25 people there to see us off. Our pastor, Bob Brunko and his wife, Donna came as well as dear friends and family. United Flight #1 to Honolulu was flying at about 38,000 feet, but WE were flying at 48,000 feet! We were flying high, but unbeknownst to us, we were about to crash!

CHAPTER FIVE

DROPPING IN

THERE I was, sitting in the line-up. Diamond Head was in my view. It was beautiful. I was actually living in Hawaii! My wife and I felt like we regularly needed to pinch ourselves.

My quiver 1981

Remember how I said a lake surfer in the ocean is like a minor league baseball athlete playing in the World Series? Well, a surfer who has never felt the raw power of a tropical Hawaiian wave is like that. I had thought the Atlantic Ocean had powerful waves but the Pacific was a whole different animal. The waves were thick and had some serious power, more than I had ever experienced.

Hawaii has powerful waves for a couple of reasons. For one, the island chain is smack dab in the middle of the ocean. It catches swells from all directions. Another reason, is that the islands are surrounded by coral reefs. When waves come up from the depths and hit the reefs, they jack up quickly and break with explosive force. I was used to crumbly waves on lake sandbars. Hawaiian waves pitched out and could send surfers to the bottom of the coral reef or break surfboards in half. It is not uncommon for there to be drownings in Hawaii when the waves get really big.

John Moline and our son Jason - North Shore Oahu. Sign reads, "Caution dangerous surf and strong riptide."

I remember my first time to surf Diamond Head Cliffs. It's a very popular break right outside of Waikiki. I was so stoked to be there. Along came a wave. I paddled for it. The view from the top of the wave to the bottom was like looking down on the Grand Canyon. The water was crystal clear and I could see straight to the bottom. There were rocks and a menacing coral reef. I was heading straight for it at breakneck speed. I freaked out! The drop was too big. I didn't think I would make it. The old saying, "he who hesitates is lost," is quite true in surfing. If you hesitate when you're going for a big wave you will almost certainly wipe out.

Well, I hesitated, and I wiped out. As I was tumbling, I felt slack on my surf leash. This meant my board had separated from the leash strapped to my ankle. I knew it would be really hard to swim in from that far out. I prayed. "Lord, if you'll help me get my board, I promise I won't try this again until I'm ready." My board hadn't gone far. I swam for it and paddled in.

Moving to Hawaii was a lot like that drop. It was really traumatic for all of us. Between homesickness, culture shock, and loneliness, we felt like we wiped out....big time.

We landed in Honolulu 9 hours from the time we took off. In that short time on the plane, both our sons got very ill. When we landed they had high fevers, upset stomachs, and strep throat. We took them to a doctor. It cost us $95. That was a small fortune to us in 1978. We were living in a rental apartment for two weeks. It was a small studio in Waikiki. While Maree nursed the boys back to health, I headed out to find us a permanent place to live.

I found an affordable two bedroom apartment that wasn't too bad. "I'll take it!" I told the realtor. He told me I had to fill out an application. I had applied for jobs before, but I never thought I would be asked to apply for a place to live. I filled it out and he added my name to a list of 50 other people who wanted that apartment! I got blisters on my feet that day, and in the days to follow, from walking around neighborhoods looking for a place to live.

Maree and I had grown up on the south side of Chicago. Racial tension between blacks and whites, were high. We both experienced race riots at our high school football games. We knew what racial prejudice was; or so we thought.

We had only experienced prejudice where whites were the majority. In Hawaii, the opposite is true. Whites are the minority. They're looked down upon by many as the people who stole Hawaii from the Hawaiians. The underlying issues are similar to the way the U.S. treated the American Indians. We were oblivious to all this, and we had never experienced racial tension from the side of the minority. That is, until now.

I kept looking for a place. I found a great house for rent in a Japanese neighborhood called Kaimuki. We thought nothing of the color difference. This wasn't Chicago, this was paradise. We thought that Japanese and haoles, the Hawaiian word for white people, weren't too far apart. We couldn't have been more wrong.

But this house had a yard! It was small but it had two bedrooms. There were two small apartments attached to it; one on the back and one on top. A Korean lady named Mrs. Kim lived in the upstairs apartment and the landlord lived in the back studio with her grown son. She was a tiny Japanese lady named Chiyo. I'll never forget our first meeting.

Me in front of Grandma Chiyo's house

The boys had been cooped up, convalescing in a tiny studio for almost two weeks. They were feeling much better and had a lot of energy to expel. We pulled up to the house. Chiyo was waiting outside for us. She was standing very straight with her arms folded across her chest. Although she was way under 5 feet tall she seemed much larger. The boys scrambled out of the car and ran around like wild animals. They were happy to be free and unrestrained. Chiyo just stared at them. She wasn't smiling.

Maree and I glanced at each other and sighed. "That's it. She hates us....a white couple with two little crazy haole boys running around her very reserved, quiet Japanese neighborhood. She spoke to Maree as she gestured toward our sons.

"Boys?" she asked. Maree nodded. "Good! Boys mo' betta!" She pounded her chest with her fist! She liked us! God gave us favor with her. The boys began calling her Grandma Chiyo and she began teaching our older son Japanese!

Grandma Chiyo with her banana tree

We missed our family and friends from our old church and neighborhood on the mainland. We tried to make friends but outside of Grandma Chiyo, making friends was hard. I remember waving at our neighbor almost every day. He didn't wave back. I kept on waving. A year later, he finally began waving to me!

One time, Maree approached a young clerk at the grocery store to ask a question. He totally ignored her and walked away. It took us awhile to figure out what was going on. The prejudice in Hawaii is just as real as anywhere else. It is just more subtle. At times we felt very discouraged but we never gave up. We knew God had called us to this place.

I'll never forget our first Christmas in the islands. It was pretty sparse. We were struggling with missing our family and all that was familiar. Spending Christmas day on the beach sounds really cool. But when you are used to snow, baking Christmas goodies in warm, snuggly kitchens, and big family gatherings, the beach soon looses its appeal.

We decided we needed to do something. We figured out that we weren't the only ones in Hawaii who were lonely at holiday time. We began seeking others out and inviting them over for special holiday celebrations. There were times we would have as many as 30 or 40 people gathered in our home. It was always local style...potluck....everybody brings something!

We finally began to make friends in the neighborhood... good friends. Our neighbors had seen a lot of people come and go over the years. They were sure we would leave, too. When we passed the one year mark, with no signs of moving, they began to open their arms of aloha to us. Those friends became friends for life.

On the ministry side of things, the Waikiki Beach Chaplaincy, (WBC), was full of opportunities. We found that the ministry was all that it was supposed to be and more.

Waikiki is a strip of land seven-tenths of a square mile long. It is located on the island of Oahu, which translates to mean "gathering place." The average daily population on this tiny strip in the ocean is over 100,000 people.

Waikiki

A Lake Surfer's Journey

There were a wide variety of ministry opportunities to choose from. The WBC held Sunday morning worship services in hotels and on the beach. They also offered ministry opportunities on the streets, in the prisons, and on the radio. They performed weddings, offered counseling, and led Bible studies during the week in varied locations on the island.

I hit the ground running! Never in my wildest dreams could I have imagined all the opportunities I would have to minister to others.

Me - preaching at Beach service

Working with the WBC in 1978 was like being a new recruit in the army. The war between light and darkness was in full swing. Everyone on staff had plenty to do. Our director, Bob Turnbull, was traveling and speaking on the mainland quite often. So, Brian Janke and I took turns preaching at the beach service.

It is hard to imagine, unless you were there. But, there I was, a relatively new Christian, with only a little ministry experience, preaching to hundreds of people on one of the most beautiful beaches in the world!

Most of the people attending those beach services planned to be there. A few did not. They would lay their beach mats down on the sand and wake up to find themselves in church! I always said that it was the only place where you can get burned and blessed at the same time!

Every Sunday many would pray to receive Jesus Christ as their personal Lord and Savior. Aloha New Testaments were given out freely. The WBC ordered them by the thousands.

The Chaplaincy's radio program aired on Sunday night on KKUA. That was the primo (number one) rock station at that time. The program consisted of 15 minutes of speaking. The station would intersperse secular songs that went along with the topic. The program was called "Son and Soul Talk."

My first program was called "The Three S's....Surf, Smoke, and Sex." I tied in my testimony sharing how God had changed my life. One of the songs the station played that night was, "Highway to Hell". As unconventional as this approach to evangelism was, it worked! Many phoned in to talk with us and pray with us to receive Christ. Then we would mail them an Aloha New Testament and a new believer's Bible study.

Beach wedding

A fellow pastor friend told me that he used to listen all the time. Of course, back in those days he would get stoned first! Even though he was high on marijuana, seeds were planted (no pun intended). Later they were watered, and then they grew. I won't mention his name, but his initials are Stephen Anthony Laudise. At the time of this writing, he is a pastor in Kailua, Hawaii. You will read more about Steve in Chapter 8. We have heard many testimonies like this one over the years.

On the streets we handed out tracts by the thousands. I used to go out by myself on Tuesday and Thursday afternoons. I tried to get believers from the local churches to come with me.

The only group I found was from First Assembly. They were radical. Sometimes, the Holy Spirit was so thick in front of the International Market Place; you could cut it with a knife! (Yeah, I know, it's not theologically correct.)

When I ran across a bunch of Y.W.A.M.er's (Youth With A Mission); my idea of street ministry would forever be changed. They brought enthusiastic worship, creative dramas and the power of the Spirit to the streets.

Over the years I met some really great people like Tom and Cindy Bauer and Foa and Marsha Fetui, team leaders with YWAM. We found that Friday nights were often the best times to be out. Along with the tourists, the streets were crowded with drug dealers, prostitutes, Hare Krishnas, pedicab drivers, and the police.

I had a heart to reach the drug dealers and users. Many times, as I walked Kalakaua Avenue, they would solicit me. I would then walk over to them and begin to tell them about Jesus. They didn't want to hear it and would run away from me. I was bummed. I decided to pray about a better approach.

The next time I was approached, the Holy Spirit took over and I found myself saying, "No thanks. I have something better." I kept on walking down the street. The dealer literally chased after me.

"Hey man, tell me what you have," he said.

"Well," I said, "I have something that gives me peace of mind."

"Go on."

"I have something that gives me freedom from guilt, forgiveness of sins and eternal life."

By now, he knew where I was going, as I ended with "I have Jesus." But I had just shared the gospel. In all my encounters during those years, I only had one drug dealer disagree with me.

"Eye has not seen, ear has not heard, neither has it entered into the heart of man, all the good things that God has in store for those who love him; but God has revealed them to us by His Spirit" (2 Corinthians 2:9-10).

As I mentioned, the Hare Krishnas were out on the streets, too. I'll never forget a guy named Showlree. We "worked" next to each other on the street. He had the best location. I didn't want to stand next to him, so I moved down the block.

One day, while reading my Bible, I came across Philippians 1:28. "Don't be intimidated by your enemies. This will be a sign to them that they are going to be destroyed, but that you are going to be saved, even by God himself." I moved back to my original location and the Krishnas ended up moving.

One time, Showlree told me that Jesus, himself, said that he was one of many ways to get to God. "In John 14:6 it's plural. Look it up," he said. Not knowing Greek, I couldn't answer him.

Jack, Gene Ozbun & Chuck Antone

Fast forward to 1981-83. We were now living in St. Paul, Minnesota and I was attending Bethel College to get my 4 year Bible degree. I know what you're thinking....Yes! It was cold!! I completed my degree and even took Greek. And then, we moved back to Hawaii.

When I got back to Hawaii, I found Showlree in Waikiki. I told him he was wrong. When Jesus said He was the way, the Greek word was 'ha hadas'. It was not only a singular noun (way), it also had a singular article (the). He never said He was one of many ways, He said He was the ONE and ONLY way.

Showlree just turned and walked away.

1983 found us back in Hawaii and back with the WBC. Bob Turnbull was no longer the director. Gene Ozbun was the head of the organization, and there were new people on staff. We were quite an eclectic group. We even opened up a Christian bookstore in Waikiki. God had created an opportunity for us to have Friday night outreach concerts right on "the Strip" in Waikiki on Kalakaua Avenue. It was an amazing location for street ministry!

In 1984, shortly after our return, Gene put me in charge of follow-up and discipleship. My job was to contact the new Christians from the beach service and other outreaches and connect them with local churches. It was a stretch for me. I had always thought of myself as strictly an evangelist. Boy, oh boy, that was about to change!

CHAPTER SIX

SOUTH SHORE...
THE BEGINNINGS

HOW did a small group of surfers, ex-drug users and drug dealers end up planting a church in Waikiki? It's quite a story....read on.

I had started out trying to change the world through evangelism. It wasn't working. We had lots of new believers, but we were finding that many of them were not growing in their faith. The few, who were growing, were the ones who got hooked up with our WBC Bible study that Gene was leading.

There, they were able to form new relationships. I began to realize that friendship, fellowship, and discipleship were needed for solid spiritual growth.

WBC staff and volunteers

After awhile, Gene felt led to step down from leading the Bible study. Everyone else on staff turned down the job. So, they asked me. The new converts that were coming wanted to and needed to attend church on Sunday. Spiritually, they had outgrown the beach service, which was basically an evangelistic outreach. Some of them were ready to raise families and wanted a church home.

It soon became very obvious to me that trying to plant these new Christians into established churches just wasn't going to happen. Many had not grown up in a church at all. Others had left behind strict, rigid church rituals. Attending a church where collared shirts, slacks, and traditional Christian music was the norm wasn't going to hack it. They needed a church where they could wear shorts, slippers, and tee-shirts. They needed to worship God just the way they were. They needed something new.

For me, growing up in the church meant wearing a suit. It was sitting in pews and singing hymns accompanied by a piano and an organ. That style of worship was great for my parents, but it chafed me like wearing a winter jacket three sizes too small in the Hawaiian summertime. I was a surfer who liked 60's rock and roll. I needed something different, too. We found it on the other side of the island.

Pastor Ralph Moore and Jack Nordgren 2007

One Sunday, Maree and I visited a church called Hope Chapel Kaneohe. They met in a high school cafeteria. As we entered the door, I noticed how everyone was dressed. It was really casual. People were wearing shorts, slippers, and tee shirts. I remember thinking that they would have all fit right in at the beach service.

My gaze drifted to the front of the room and I couldn't believe my eyes. There were drums and electric guitars and a lot of energetic people belting out praises to God. The worship rocked. The pastor got up to speak. He was wearing blue jeans.

When Pastor Ralph Moore opened his mouth, he shared his vision of planting churches in Hawaii. Their goal was to reach 1% of Hawaii's population in 10 years. That added up to be around 11,000 people. I thought to myself that either Pastor Ralph was totally nuts, or he had heard from God. (By the way, we didn't reach the goal in 10 years, but we did reach it in 11).

Maree and I both felt this Hope Chapel thing was the way to go. I contacted Ralph about starting a Hope Chapel in Waikiki. Ralph liked our vision for planting a church there. I started making plans to transition the Bible study group into a Hope Chapel.

I didn't know it then, but whenever there is a change in pastoral leadership in a church, the second pastor is usually chewed up and spit out by the congregation. I was no exception.

The Bible study grew from 30 people down to 12 under my anointed leadership. After that brief period of phenomenal church growth, we moved into the Waikiki Community Center and started Hope Chapel South Shore. We started out meeting on Sunday evenings because I was still on the beach with the WBC in the mornings.

We were a ragtag group, but then so were the twelve disciples. They consisted of a tax collector, fishermen, a zealot, a thief, and various others. They should have been called the dirty dozen, not the twelve disciples.

Our group was not much different from them. A very motley crew assembled that first night in the Waikiki Community Center Chapel! There was Glenn Morgan and his roommate Rich. There were two young couples: Mark & Laurie and Rapheal & Chris. They came to us through the beach service. Then of course, there was our family: Jack, Maree, Jason, Joshua, and little did we know, nine months later, Josiah.

Jack and Josiah

Maree and Josiah

On that day Hope Chapel South Shore was born. The Bible says in Zechariah to "despise not small beginnings." We didn't.

Raphael had a very interesting testimony. He had moved to Hawaii from Florida. He had been in a family business with his father. They were smuggling cocaine from Colombia. The police were after them and Raphael split. While hitchhiking across the country he had a divine appointment. A seminary student picked him up and led him to the Lord.

Upon reaching Hawaii, Raphael got into surfing and soon took up his old drug habits. One day, as he crossed the beach to get to the surf, he stumbled upon the beach service. He sat down on the sand to listen. As he heard the message of the gospel again; he recommitted his life to the Lord.

Throughout the years of ministry, there was one lesson I needed to learn over and over about the grace of God. I'll never forget the time God used Raphael to re-teach it to me.

Hope Chapel South Shore worship service 1985

One night, we were getting ready for our worship service in the chapel. Raphael was helping me to set up the chairs. A local guy wandered in. He reeked of pakalolo (marijuana). To say that his eyes were bloodshot would be an understatement. This guy was so out of it he didn't even know where he was.

I remember thinking, "Man, this guy is a real loser." Just as I began to think that thought, Raphael walked by me. Under his breath I heard him say, "There but for the grace of God, go I." The spirit in which he said it communicated not only his thankfulness to God, but, also his hope for this lost individual. I was humbled.

I realized that we all were like this man in God's eyes... reeking from sin, blinded, confused, and disoriented. Only the transforming power of God allows us to really see. We would find many people like this guy over the years and witness to them about the love of Jesus.

And so our journey began....the most frustrating, disappointing, exciting, and rewarding 22 years of our lives.

Laurie Piper dances hula at HCSS first retreat

CHAPTER SEVEN

THE GREATEST ALOHA

THE Hawaiian word 'Aloha' is often misunderstood. Most people know that it means 'hello,' 'good-bye', and even 'love.' Those are all correct. But its meaning goes much deeper. Aloha is actually a compound word. 'Alo' means face. 'Ha' means breath. When the old Hawaiians would greet one another they would put their foreheads together while saying this beautiful word, and share the breath of life.

God sent Jesus into the world to die on the cross for our sins. He did this so that he could send His Spirit (His breath) into our lives. He shared His aloha with us first. "God showed how much He loved us by sending His only Son into the world so that we might have eternal life through Him. This is real love. It is not that we loved God, but that he loved us and sent His Son as a sacrifice to take away our sins" (1 John 4:9-10).

Ray and Jack - HCSS baptism

I first learned about this kind of love from my father as a boy. My dad used to say, "I'll always love you, son." I was a smart-aleck teenager who had a wise-crack for everything. So, one day I asked him, "What if I were to kill somebody? What would you do then?" His answer was, "Well, then, I'll visit you, and love you, in jail."

My dad always loved me no matter what. He taught me that God loved anybody and everybody. God still wants to share His aloha with everyone. "But God showed His great love for us by sending Christ to die for us while we were still sinners" (Romans 5:8).

Hope Chapel South Shore was given a nickname that reflected this kind of Aloha. Amongst some of the community we were know as "the garbage church."

We'd share God's aloha with anyone. We didn't care if people were homeless, drug dealers, strippers, transsexuals, homosexuals, or AIDS victims. We loved them all.

Let me tell you about a guy named Jeff. It was 1985. I was leaving my office at the community center when I met Jeff. He was coming out of the Waikiki Health Center. We met briefly and went our separate ways.

The next day there was a knock on my office door. Jeff was standing there, visibly shaken. I looked into his eyes. They were filled with fear.

"I got it!" he said.

"Got what?" was my reply.

"AIDS."

My mind was racing. I was trying to remember all the stuff I had read. Remember, this was 1985. Could I catch AIDS from this guy? Some "Christian" books I had read were saying just that. There were even churches that would not allow people with this disease into their worship services.

That's when the Holy Spirit reminded me of the story of Jesus and the leper in Mark 1. "Jesus was filled with compassion and He reached out and touched the man." I grabbed Jeff and hugged him tight. He sobbed.

After several minutes he calmed down. He talked. I listened. He shared his life story. I shared with him that God loved him and wanted a relationship with him.

He prayed with me and asked Jesus to forgive his sins and come into his life. He received God's aloha. He was a changed young man. His fear turned to faith.

We became good friends over the next several years before God took him home. As the disease progressed, he went back home to California for medical care. His mom moved there too.

Later, she shared with me about her last visit with him in the hospital. She was alone and standing by his bedside. He looked up and asked, "Mom, who are all these people with you?" She was confused. She told him that she didn't see anyone else there.

Jeff died the next day. It was then she realized that God had sent His angels. They had come to take her son home. I'm sure the first words he heard were, "Aloha Jeff. Welcome home."

HCSS church on the beach – Willard, David, Dennis and Joey

God gave us another opportunity to share His Aloha. It was Sunday evening. We were having our regular worship service. I was in the middle of my sermon when 5 girls came in and sat in the back row. There was something unusual about those gals and I couldn't quite put my finger on it. They left quickly as the service ended.

Our associate pastor helped me to figure it out. Those gals weren't girls. They were males dressed as females. They were transvestites. We didn't know what to call them, so we nicknamed them "the angels."

The next Sunday they came back. As I ended the service I heard the Holy Spirit say to me, "Go hug them and share My aloha."

"No way, Lord, they'll think I'm nuts."

"Go hug them."

"No way, Lord. They'll think I'm gay."

"Go hug them."

I obeyed. As I hugged each of them, I told them it was a $50 fine if they left without getting a hug. I hugged them every Sunday for a year. Then they stopped coming. We didn't see them again but we had done what God wanted us to do. We shared His Aloha.

About 2 years later, while my family and I were off island on vacation something amazing happened. Dennis, our associate pastor, was leading the service. Some members from Teen Challenge were sharing in our service that day.

Teen Challenge is a Christian recovery program for those seeking to get clean from alcohol and drug abuse. They sang and shared their powerful testimonies. After the service a young man came up to Dennis. "Don't you remember me?" Dennis thought he did, but wasn't sure. "You used to know me. I was one of "the angels".

He had come to know Christ as his Lord and Savior and accept himself as God made him. God's Aloha is powerful.

Jack and Dennis pray before baptism

Speaking of powerful Aloha, here is another example. My phone rang. It was Gene and Shellaine, a young couple who had been attending our church for almost 2 years. "We need to talk to you," they said.

Shel had been working as a waitress at Bubba Gumps Restaurant. She met a guy there named Mike. Mike played on our worship team. He invited her to Hope Chapel. She came and brought her husband, Gene. Every time they came Shel would cry throughout the whole service. She didn't know it, but God's spirit was tugging at her heart, big time. After just a little while, both of them asked Jesus into their lives. They were baptized in the ocean off Waikiki Beach. God began to breathe His Aloha into their lives.

Even before they came to Hope Chapel, and to Jesus, God had performed a huge miracle in Shel's life. She had been healed of cancer through holistic treatments and God's healing power. She had also been healed of endometriosis. Her doctor had wanted to perform a hysterectomy because of the damage and the pain she was in. She refused and they resorted to prayer.

She wanted children but the doctor said the scar tissue was too great. They prayed. We prayed. She was not only healed, but God gave them twins...a boy and a girl. They named the boy Golden and their daughter is named Jetta. Life was good.... or was it?

Now, here they were, sitting in our living room looking very somber and serious. We had no idea what they were about to tell us.

"We are wanted by the law in Las Vegas," they said. They proceeded to tell us one of the most amazing stories we had ever heard.

Eight years earlier they were both addicted to crystal meth. Gene had been arrested, tried, and convicted for burglary in Vegas. He was awaiting sentencing and looking at 3-10 years in prison.

Shel had also been arrested and charged when they decided to flee to Florida. They began to live just under the radar. Driving a car was a huge risk for them. Getting a ticket would mean an arrest because of their warrants. They had to pay cash for everything. Opening a checking account could lead the police to their whereabouts.

In 1999 they moved to the Islands and lived on Kauai. After 7 months they moved to Oahu. They had been running for over 5 years.

They continued their secret lives. It was getting more and more difficult. They missed their families desperately. They had not spoken with any of them in all that time. Neither of their families knew about the birth of their twins.

One day, on a whim, Shel went online and typed in her name. A website appeared from her family. They were pleading to know anything at all about her.

She nearly fell apart. She had no idea her family still loved and cared about her. The absence from her family was tearing her up. She and Gene prayed about it long and hard. Then they came to us.

Gene & Shel

A Lake Surfer's Journey

"We want to turn ourselves in," they said. They had no idea how we or the rest of the church would react when they confessed. They were scared. They were afraid we would ask them to leave the church because they had been living a lie.

Jetta and Golden

Being asked to leave might have happened in another church, but this was Hope Chapel South Shore! We hugged them and assured them of our Aloha.

They had no idea what was going to happen. They both thought that they might have to go to prison. That would mean being away from their twins for a long time. There were a lot of tears and a lot of prayers. We told them we would stand by them and even go to court with them.

They moved back to Vegas to reunite with their families and turn themselves in. Shel's case was immediately thrown out by the court, much to everyone's relief. But Gene's situation was way more serious. We arrived in Vegas the day before his court date. Everyone was hoping and praying for the best, but trying to prepare for the worst.

Josh at "Canoes"

On the morning of the trial, Maree and I saw a rainbow. We actually thought nothing of it. We saw rainbows all the time in Hawaii. Maree stayed behind at the hotel to care for the twins so that Shel could be in court with Gene. I went down to the courthouse to be a support.

The case just before had us worried. It was similar to Gene's. The man was given a year in prison. He was handcuffed and shackled. As he was led out of the courtroom, Shel began to cry. Gene's name was called.

He was given a chance to speak. He admitted to his past crimes and asked for forgiveness. His lawyer pointed out that there were many family members and friends in the courtroom to support him....even his pastor from Hawaii.

We all held our breath and prayed as we waited for the judge to speak. He told us that he had received 52 letters of support from Gene's friends and family.

He then turned and spoke to the other prisoners in the courtroom. He proceeded to use Gene as an example of someone who could turn his life around. He gave Gene 2 years probation and a $2000 fine.

We emptied into the hallway where hugs and tears flowed. God had done another miracle for Gene and Shel and we had been there to witness it!

As we left the courthouse the rainbow was still there...in a cloudless sky! It was then that we were told how rare rainbows are in Vegas. We felt it was God's way of confirming this miracle for Gene and Shel.

In Acts 10:34-35 it says, "After being divinely lead to the house of the Gentile centurion, Cornelius, Peter said, 'I now realize how true it is that God does not show favoritism but accepts men from every nation who fear him and do what is right.'"

Aloha Ke Akua means God's love. Aloha Ke Akua is for everyone who will receive it. This kind of love was demonstrated through Christ's death on the cross. When we ask for forgiveness for our sins and ask Jesus into our lives, He comes in. God breathes into us His life. Shel and Gene had asked for God's love and forgiveness, and God had given it to them in spades!

It was our first time in Vegas. As our plane lifted off the runway, back to Honolulu, we felt like we had just won a million dollar jackpot!

❧

CHAPTER EIGHT

MAKING WAVES

ONE sunny morning I was having one of my daily "dawn patrol" surf sessions at Canoe's in Waikiki. It was a small day, and there were long waits between the sets. A bunch of the regulars were "talking story"- just talking about anything that came to mind and catching up. It was starting to get boring when someone yelled to my friend. "Hey! Kaleo, do a cannon ball and make some waves!" Kaleo Prescott is a really fun loving guy; a real jokester and the life of any party. He is over 50 years old, but going on 15. Well, true to form, Kaleo jumped off his board and did an almost perfect cannon ball. I held up my hands and gave him a score of "9". Others were laughing and doing the same. He got some pretty good scores.

Kaleo, Rick & ??????

All of a sudden, we saw a huge wave on the outside. Kaleo and I paddled out as fast as we could. It was the biggest, best wave of the day. I wish I could tell you we caught it but in our exuberance, we paddled out too far.

We missed it and everyone else caught it. I usually leave that last part of the story out but Kaleo always reminds me to tell it all!

Obviously Kaleo's cannon ball didn't generate the wave we tried to catch that day, but there is a deeper principle to be learned. God has used the Hope Chapels to make waves in Hawaii and all over the world.

They start churches everywhere by raising up and releasing leaders. Luke 6:38 says, "Give, and it will be given to you. A good measure, pressed down, shaken together and running over, will be poured into your lap. For with the measure you use, it will be measured to you."

I'd been used to churches and ministries trying to hold on to people. There was little releasing into other places or areas to serve. The mentality was always to hold onto the "good people." However, from Pastor Ralph Moore, I've learned to do the opposite.

Dawn patrol - Rick Chin – Hawaii

When Hope Chapel Kaneohe was only about a year old, they sent out over 100 of their best people to start a church 4 miles down the road in Kahalu. I was stunned. I'd never seen anything like that before. Losing that many people from a congregation could kill a church. God honored the obedience of Hope Chapel Kaneohe. It is now one of the largest churches in Hawaii continuing to release people and plant new churches.

This principle has always stuck with me. I'll never forget the time when my good friend Bill told me he wanted to start a Messianic Jewish congregation. Bill and his family had been attending Hope Chapel South Shore for a year. We had become good friends. Bill and his wife Marcy were great workers. They knew the Word and were doing some great ministry at our church.

I can't say I didn't struggle with releasing him but Ralph's example had impacted me. We did what we could to help them get started. Bill started his Messianic church and last I heard it is still thriving there.

Bill has since moved on and is now a missionary in Israel. He found a good replacement for his congregation in Hawaii and they still meet on Saturday mornings in the Waikiki Community Center's Chapel.

Let me tell you about another guy named Stephen Anthony Laudise. Steve was a rocker. He had been playing guitar since he was a teenager. His dream was to be a rock star. In the 1970's he used to get stoned on marijuana and listen to the Waikiki Beach Chaplaincy's "Soul Talk" on the radio. Eventually he became a Christian and started playing for the real Rock; our Lord Jesus Christ. He would play his guitar in the prison, on the streets, and in the church. He shared his faith anywhere he could.

I met Steve back in 1983 when I was still on staff with the Waikiki Beach Chaplaincy. We would do outreach concerts together on the streets of wild, wicked, but wonderful Waikiki. We would set up our sound system right across the street from a porn shop. The customers would come running across busy Kalakaua Avenue to hear the rock music. The managers of the place used to call the cops to harass us because we were bad for their business!

On Sunday nights we ministered together in the Pearl Harbor Brig. Steve was so entertaining that over half of the prisoners in the prison would come to hear him play. There was a tremendous anointing on Steve as he played his guitar and talked with the guys.

Steve is a very funny guy. He does great impressions and makes up jokes on the spot. Sometimes he'd get me and the prisoners laughing so hard, we'd nearly cry. Throughout these times of ministry we became good friends. Many of the prisoners gave their hearts to the Lord.

Eventually Steve joined me on staff at the Chaplaincy. I left six months later to start Hope Chapel South Shore. We'd often joke that Steve was following me. First, he followed me to the streets, to the Brig, and then to join the staff. He continued to follow me, sort of....

He was asked to be the worship leader at a new church plant called Aikahi Christian Fellowship. Shortly after, the senior pastor resigned and Steve became the pastor. He changed the name of the church to Hope Chapel Kailua.

When Steve became a pastor, his worship band had an awesome drummer named Bill Youngs. Bill and his wife JoJo were long time friends of Steve and his wife Dawn. In fact, they were actually the ones who lead Steve and Dawn to the Lord. Shortly after Steve joined the Chaplaincy staff, Bill came on board.

Jack & Bill Youngs 1993

Bill was as radical for Jesus as Steve was. Or maybe it was the other way around. Over the years all three of us became close friends and brothers in the Lord. No matter how much time goes by in between visits or phone calls we can always pick up right where we left off.

At one time our church needed a worship leader for our Sunday evening service. I asked Bill if he would help us out and he said yes. Those Sunday evenings became awesome times of worship. Bill was picking up the guitar fast and he became an amazing worship leader.

I'll never forget the time we were in the car heading out for a surf session. Bill said, "I have this idea for a worship song." He began singing and playing air guitar. I was blown away by the song and told him he should play it in church. He did.

That was just the first of many, many worship songs that he's written over the years. Of all the songs I've heard, though, that first song, "You're my Rock" is still my favorite.

Things were going along real well. Hope Chapel South Shore was growing. We had great volunteers, a great staff, and awesome worship. Then, one day Bill came to me and said, "God wants me to plant a church in Waimanalo.

Once again; I struggled with letting someone go. Once again, I remembered Ralph Moore's example to let go; knowing it's not about building our kingdom. It's about building His kingdom

Bill and his family left HCSS and started Lighthouse Christian Fellowship. Here's the interesting part. We provided the pastor, but Steve released people from his church to help Bill get started.

These two church plants can be traced back to Ralph's influence on me and my influence on Steve and Bill. Of course, the influence ultimately originated from God and His magnificent cannonball splash when He sent Jesus to die for our sins.

Bill Youngs leading worship at
Lighthouse Christian Fellowship

Hope Chapel South Shore Board Meeting
Trevor, Jack, Kaleo and Danny

Jesus said, "I will build my church and the gates of hell will not prevail against it".

CHAPTER NINE

HAWAIIAN BEACH BOY

WHEN we hear the words beach boy, most of us think of the popular music group from the 60's. A beach boy living in Hawaii is much different. Hawaiian beach boys work on the beach. They are the ones who give surf lessons and canoe rides to anyone who wants to learn. Their traditions and culture of life go back many years. The ancient Hawaiian arts of fishing, canoeing, surfing, swimming, spear fishing, free diving, and weather forecasting without technology, are still passed down from generation to generation. They are known for spreading Aloha and their love of the ocean. Many of them are true watermen. They are men who know the ocean like the back of their hand. For them, the ocean is life

The old timers are treasures. They share stories of how it used to be. They tell stories about Duke Kahanamoku. He was the father of modern surfing and the most famous beach boy of all time. They also tell stories about his brothers and many others. Their names are revered by the young and the old. I have become really close friends with one Hawaiian beach boy in particular.

Photo by Mandee Converse

HCSS board meeting – Dennis, Jack and Moose

It all started in 1984 when the rent on our townhouse went up $250. I was freaking out. Back then we had two sons. Jason was 10 and Joshua was almost 9. Our third son, Josiah, was on the way. We were living hand to mouth... God's hand to our mouth.

I prayed really hard. I argued with God. "What are you doing, God? You know we can't afford this rent increase."

I frantically began to look for another place to live. I found one. God led me to another town home. The increase would only be $50 a month. It was in the same complex we were already living in. We didn't even have to rent a truck to move our stuff.

Romans 8:28 tells us that, "All things work together for good for those who love the Lord and are called according to his purpose." It would take me a number of years before I would realize how God worked our rent increase for good.

We moved in next to a single mom and her two keiki (children). We quickly became friends. Our boys would often baby sit for her. There were several times that she needed someone to watch her kids in an emergency.

I remember meeting their dad. His name was Dennis Sallas. He was a beach boy. He worked for the City and County as a lifeguard. His kids adored him but he didn't come around much. He wasn't a very involved dad.

Dennis was well known in Hawaii. In his college years, he was a star athlete for the University of Hawaii. Now, he was just another beach boy using drugs and being an absent father. I thought he was a bum but God didn't.

One time, our family was headed out the door to the movies. That was actually a kind of rare treat for us, so the boys were very excited. There was a knock on the door. It was our neighbor and she was in tears.

Dennis was supposed to watch her kids so she could go to work. He hadn't shown up. He hadn't called. She was late for work. She needed our help. We tried not to show our disappointment. There was no question about what we would do. She was our friend.

Over the years I prayed for them. I told God how to handle things. "Well, Lord, the mom is nice. Could you change her first? Then, Lord, the kids are pretty cute. They need You, too. Maybe if they come to know you; just maybe the dad will come, too. Amen."

Dennis playing ukulele

Well, I've learned a few things since that time. First, there is a God. And second, I'm not Him.

God did change this family, but He did it His way; not mine.

Here's how it happened. I was visiting Hope Chapel Kaneohe's Friday night service. I was talking with Pastor Ralph when I saw someone familiar out of the corner of my eye. It was Dennis. I pointed to him and said to Ralph, "There is the biggest miracle I've ever seen! I never thought I'd see him at church!"

Dennis recognized me and walked over to ask me a question. "I need a Bible. Which one do you think I should get?"

I was in shock! I managed to mumble, "I think the Life Application Bible, NIV version is the best".

To be honest, I didn't really think he was going to get a Bible, let alone read it. I was wrong.

About a year later, Dennis walked into our Sunday worship service in Waikiki. He had his two kids with him and a Life Application NIV Bible. He had come to know Jesus Christ as his personal Lord and Savior.

He started bringing his children to church. They knew our sons. Remember, they had been their babysitters. By now, Jason and Joshua were leading worship. That is why his kids wanted to come to Hope Chapel South Shore.

Jason, Josiah & Joshua

That Sunday was the first of many. He not only brought his children, he himself began attending Bible studies. To my amazement, when we opened things up for discussion, he knew what he was talking about. I knew he had been reading that Bible. He began to pastor.

I've never seen anyone grow as quickly as he did. He began the painful process of reconciling with the rest of his children...eight in all. His passion for God, his family and friends was inspiring.

In time, he began to take over some pastoral responsibilities. He began to lead small groups. He eventually started preaching at the Sunday evening services.

Dennis and his friends, Willard Harvest, and Joey Akaka, came up with an idea. They wanted to hold an Easter Sunrise service on Waikiki Beach. I gave them my blessing. They enlisted the help of others from church. It started small, but grew with each year. Now, the annual event is attended by several thousand people! Hundreds have prayed to receive the Lord over the years and many have been baptized.

Easter Sunrise service 2003; Joey, Willard and Dennis

I've got to tell you that I've never seen anything like it. Ever since 1978, I'd had a desire to see God pour out His Spirit over Waikiki.

I've seen it. It happens on Easter Sunday morning, at sunrise, on the Hula mound, right on the beach in the heart of Waikiki.

Pastor Dennis preaching at Easter sunrise service

In 2006, an elderly lady came up to me after the service and told me she wanted to hear Pastor Dennis preach more. I told her she would because I was going on vacation and Dennis would be preaching both morning services for me. That wasn't good enough for her. She wanted him to preach every Sunday, even when I returned.

Needless to say, I got a bit defensive. After some prayer and a long talk with her and my friend, Jim Baldwin; I came up with a solution. Pastor Dennis would preach at the 8:30 a.m. service. I would preach at the 10:30.

I didn't realize it at the time, but God was preparing Dennis, Hope Chapel, and me for some major changes

Jack performing Dennis and Donna's wedding

CHAPTER TEN

SAY "COWABUNGA"
TO MICHIGAN

I T was a summer day in July, 2007. I pulled up to the beach. I looked at the surf. Lines upon lines were peeling off. There were over 20 surfers out, already. I took my board off the car and ran down to the water. It wasn't my first time to surf Ersula's, one of the most popular breaks in the area.

(King) Kenny Carlson, Ersula's, St. Joe, Michigan

Photo by Clay Carlson

I was glad to see so many familiar faces as I paddled out. Steve, Jim, Ryan, Jonas, Mark, Roman, and Mike were there. The Carlson brothers joined me, too. Ace-King-Goum (Clay) was there in the morning and King Kenny came in the afternoon. The waves were great. The water was warm and I surfed until I could not surf anymore. I was 'surfed out'.

I wasn't in Hawaii. I was in St. Joe, Michigan. God had called and I said, "Cowabunga"- let's go for it... to Michigan.

In Hawaii I had the best job in the whole world. I was the pastor of a church in Waikiki. A typical morning for me started with "dawn patrol board meeting" at Canoe's.

This meant getting up before the sun rose and going surfing at one of the best long board breaks on the south shore. Getting to know the guys in the water and being a witness for Jesus was just icing on the cake. Devotions and fellowship followed at Seattle's Best coffee shop. Then I went into work at the Hope Chapel office. It was only one block away.

I love to surf and I love to pastor. Why in the world would I ever want to leave Hawaii?

For the past couple of years I'd had this strange feeling. I felt like I was supposed to be somewhere else. I didn't know where.

I still enjoyed being a pastor. I still enjoyed surfing. I even had the opportunity to surf in several contests and win a couple. Hawaii is probably the only place in the world where a surf contest would have a division for pastors.

Photo by Rob Santanello

Surf Contest-Waikiki: Pastor Jack, Pastor Richard & Pastor Elwin

A Lake Surfer's Journey

I had so many fond memories in Hawaii. Our family had so much history here. We had made many close friends. It would be impossible to leave...unless God called us to.

In January 2006, my father went home to be with the Lord. He was a godly man who had a great influence on me. He read his Living Bible through 27 times. He lived what he read.

My dad was very ill and had been in a lot of pain. He wanted to go home to be with Jesus and leave his suffering behind. His funeral was the happiest, saddest event of my whole life.

Photo by Jack Nordgren

Paul Gregory (Moose) at Ersula's – St. Joe, Michigan

Maree and I flew to Michigan for the funeral. Our three sons joined us there. We all stayed together at the King and Queen's castle (Ken and Dianne Carlson's home). They lived in Bridgman, Michigan.

It was the first time me, Maree, and our sons had all been together in five years. Our two older sons had married and moved their families to the mainland. We had a great time hanging out and reminiscing about Dad.

Maree's "J-men" at Bethany Beach; Jason, Josiah, Joshua & Jack

It was during this time that the Lord began speaking to my wife and me about Bridgman. We both felt God was calling us to plant a church there. My mom was living there; but other than that we had no reason to move there.

Our lives were in Hawaii. We both began to pray. The more we prayed, the more convinced we were that Bridgman was where we were supposed to be.

I shared this with a close friend. He began to pray about it. We sought the Lord's direction in His Word. He kept confirming it over and over.

All of a sudden, things began to make sense. God had been preparing Pastor Dennis to take over Hope Chapel in Waikiki. He was ready. We had been away from family and friends on the mainland for years. Now, we could reconnect. God had placed that unsettled feeling in my heart. It was time to move on.

"Delight yourself in the Lord and He shall give you the desires of your heart. Commit your way to the Lord and He will do it" (Psalm 37:4, 5). God had given me the desires of my heart and brought me to Hawaii.

Now, he was doing it again. He was giving me the desires of my heart. He was bringing me home to Michigan.

Let me share with you just one of the ways God confirmed this new call on our lives. It happened in August, 2006. We had just arrived at a rest stop on the toll road in Illinois. We were headed to Michigan to search for a house.

We had stopped for a bite to eat and our hearts and minds were racing as we tried to figure out the 'what's, where's, why's, and how's' of our lives. Did we really hear from God about moving to Michigan? What if we didn't? Will He still take care of us? What if we don't find a house? How are we going to move our things across the ocean? What should we bring? What should we leave behind?

What will happen to our son, Josiah, who is not moving with us? What if we sell our house in Hawaii but can't find one in Bridgman? What if we find a house in Bridgman but can't sell our house in Hawaii? These were just a few of the many thoughts that were swirling around in our heads when a miracle came to our table.

"Do you need prayer?" she asked. The comforting voice broke through our anxious, troubled thoughts. We looked up to see a pleasant looking woman in her late 60's or early 70's. She was smiling at us as we nodded our heads 'yes' in answer to her question.

"God sent me over to pray for you and also to tell you this... the Lord wants you to know that He is with you." she said. Tears sprang to my wife's eyes as she looked at me. I wondered if this lady was an angel.

We held hands. It wasn't a long prayer and to tell you the truth, I really don't remember the exact words she used. What I do know, is her words touched those places of fear, indecision, and uncertainty. God gave us the faith boost we needed to carry on. We finished our meal with lighter hearts and headed on to Michigan.

Photo by Diane Carlson

Jack at Ersula's

We had left Hope Chapel in the capable hands of Pastor Dennis during this time. He called us twice. The first phone call was to share about his family reunion.

They held it on the beach. One of his relatives approached him about baptizing his 8 year old daughter. Dennis shared the gospel with her and led her in prayer to receive Christ as her Lord and Savior. Then he guided her down to the ocean to be baptized.

As they were coming out of the water, three more of his relatives were waiting to be baptized. Dennis went through the process of explaining the gospel and praying again, and again, and again. By the end of the day, over 20 of his relatives had prayed to receive the Lord and had gotten baptized! It was a strong confirmation to me and Maree that we had the right man to take over Hope Chapel South Shore!

Photo by Clay Carlson

Jack at Ersula's

Dennis' second call was to inform us that there had been 6 visitors in the Sunday morning worship service. That really didn't surprise us. We'd had visitors nearly every Sunday. But as far as we could remember, we had never had visitors from this place. They just happened to be from a small town in Michigan called Bridgman!

Proverbs 4:11 (L.B. translation) was my Dad's favorite verse. It says, "I would have you learn this one great fact; that a life of doing right is the wisest life there is." I believe the happiest and most contented any of us can ever be is when we are where God wants us and willing to do what He wants us to do.

Surf Contest-Waikiki: Jack surfing in Pastor's division

Waikiki is a strip of land running along the Pacific Ocean on the island of Oahu. It's only 7/10's of a square mile. The average population is over 100,000 on any given day of the year. The average stay of a resident is only 6 months. Most of its inhabitants are tourists.

Waikiki was a place where the Hawaiian kings and queens gathered to vacation many, many years ago. It's the place where surfing was born. It's a place of activity 24 hours a day, 7 days a week. It never sleeps, and the lights of this city burn all night, 365 days a year.

In contrast, Bridgman, Michigan has only about 2,400 people. There's only one traffic light in the town. It has a beach, called WEKO Beach, which is deserted 9 months out of the year. It's a slow way of life in Bridgman.

What do Waikiki and Bridgman have in common? They both have people who need Jesus. What else do they have in common? I guess that would be us!

EPILOGUE

by Maree Nordgren

O N March 6, 2007, we arrived in Bridgman, Michigan. When people find out we used to live in Hawaii they inevitably ask this question, "Why did you leave Hawaii?"

SSF worship team

Our short answer is, "Remember Jonah and the whale? Well, we didn't want to get swallowed by a big fish." (If you don't know this story, God told Jonah to go to Nineveh. Jonah sailed away in the opposite direction. He was swallowed by a big fish. In the belly of that fish he changed his mind. Then he decided to go where God told him.)

SSF worship service

If they want to know more, we tell them that for 30 years God has been guiding us and leading us. He led us to Hawaii and now he has led us to Michigan. How could we NOT go?

On November 4, 2007 South Shore Fellowship was officially born. We are meeting at the Lion's Café at Weko Beach in Bridgman. Yes, I said 'beach'. It is a beautiful location no matter what the season. God has brought us full circle. We are still on the beach and have one of the most beautiful views of Lake Michigan around.

Because of the café setting, we have a unique casual style. People gather around the tables and enjoy coffee and treats while Pastor Jack brings us our spiritual food!

We are not a traditional church but we worship the same Jesus. We have a contemporary style of worship using guitars, keyboards, and drums. Jack's "pulpit" is an old surfboard that has been cut down, painted, re-glassed and revamped. It's gnarly! (Thanks to Ryan Beck.)

South Shore Fellowship exists for one reason. Our slogan is, "It's all about relationships!"

Our God is a relational God. He created us to fellowship with Him and with each other. If we can get people excited about knowing God and relating to Him and others, in a personal way, then we have done our job.

Josh Nordgren at WEKO on Waikiki Jack's SUP board

September 2009 - Jack dropping in at Lincoln Township, Michigan

And so, we are back at the beach. We are sharing Christ's love with people. We are training up leaders and trusting Him to grow His church. Jack has even been working part time with Ryan Gerad at Third Coast Surf Shop giving surf lessons. (Some things never change!) And now he has even opened up his own beach stand at WEKO. It's called Waikiki Jack's (http://waikikijacks.com/). Stop by Memorial day through Labor Day 11-6 PM (closed Mondays). We hope our church can stay in this beautiful location at WEKO Beach. We don't know what the future holds, but we know who holds the future.

September 2009 - Jack goes backside at Lincoln Township

2007

Photo by Jason Gerod

2009

It's all about relationships!

For more info:
on us: **www.southshorefellowship.org**
on Hope Chapel South Shore: **www.hopechapelwaikiki.org**
on Great Lakes Surf Shop: **www.thirdcoastsurfshop.com**
on Waikiki Jack's: **www.waikikijacks.com**

Also available is Pastor Jack's *S.U.R.F Journal: How to Have Daily Surf Sessions with God (Volume 1)*

For more about the author, news on upcoming projects and discussions, please go to: http://bit.ly/jack-nordgren

Made in the USA
Charleston, SC
12 August 2015